The NatureTrail Book of
WOODLANDS

The NatureTrail Book of WOODLANDS

Introduction

Of all the different parts of the countryside, woodlands provide one of the richest areas for wildlife. Animals of all shapes and sizes can feed, shelter, breed, and make their homes in woods, partly because of the huge variety of plant life which many woods contain.

Even the rotting logs and leaf litter on the woodland floor attract countless tiny creatures, and these in their turn provide food for many larger animals.

This book explains how all the animals and plants in a wood form a living community. As well as helping you to identify what you see, it will help you to understand how woodland animals and plants survive.

It also gives you lots of tips on how to explore woods yourself, and suggests ways of finding out more about these fascinating places.

The picture on the left shows a wood which contains trees called Sessile Oaks. It looks, at first glance, rather empty. In the same way, if you enter a real wood, you may feel that there is not much there to see.

However, if you sit quietly and wait patiently, the animals will gradually come out of hiding.

Every wood is different, so the animals you see will depend on the type of wood you are in. This book describes the main types of wood to look for and the kind of wildlife you may find there.

Contents

Acknowledgements

Written by Barbara Cork and Helen Gilks

Special consultants Dr Keith Kirby, M.I.For. Michael Chinery

Edited by Sue Jacquemier

Designed by David Bennett

Research by Anna Makowiecka

Illustrators
Bob Bampton (Garden Studio)
Denise Finney
Sheila Galbraith
Ian Jackson
Tricia Newell
Chris Shields (Wilcock Riley)

Additional illustrations by
Sue Camm
Coral Guppy (John Martin Artists)
Caroline McLean
Sam Thompson

Printed in Belgium by
CASTERMAN, S.A., Tournai.

First published in 1981 by Usborne Publishing Ltd, 20 Garrick Street, London WC2E 9BJ
© 1981 by Usborne Publishing Limited

Exploring woodlands

The best way to explore a wood is to walk slowly and quietly and look very carefully all around you. Don't expect to see everything in just one visit. Most of the birds and other animals will move away or hide as soon as they hear you coming, so it is a good idea to sit quietly in one place for a few hours.

Draw and make notes about the plants and animals you discover, and use this book to find out more about them.

It can also be very interesting to compare one type of wood with another. Or you could choose a small corner of a wood and visit it regularly over a year to see how it changes.

What to take with you

Here are some ideas for things to take with you when you go exploring. Try to wear dull colours, such as green or brown, as they will help you to merge into the background. You do not need to take everything shown here – the most important things to take with you are a notebook, a pencil and a sharp pair of eyes.

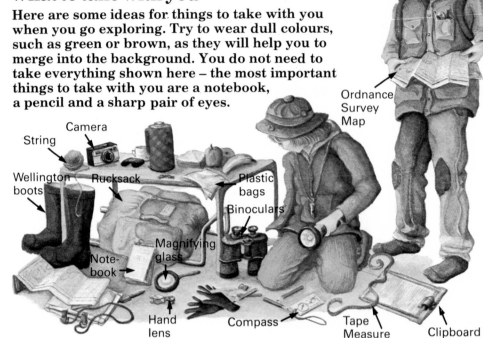

Ordnance Survey Map
String
Camera
Wellington boots
Rucksack
Plastic bags
Binoculars
Magnifying glass
Note-book
Hand lens
Compass
Tape Measure
Clipboard

TRACKS AND SIGNS

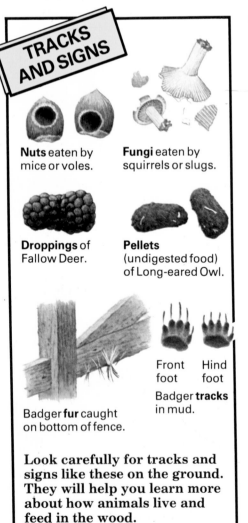

Nuts eaten by mice or voles.

Fungi eaten by squirrels or slugs.

Droppings of Fallow Deer.

Pellets (undigested food) of Long-eared Owl.

Front foot

Hind foot

Badger tracks in mud.

Badger fur caught on bottom of fence.

Look carefully for tracks and signs like these on the ground. They will help you learn more about how animals live and feed in the wood.

Where to look for wildlife

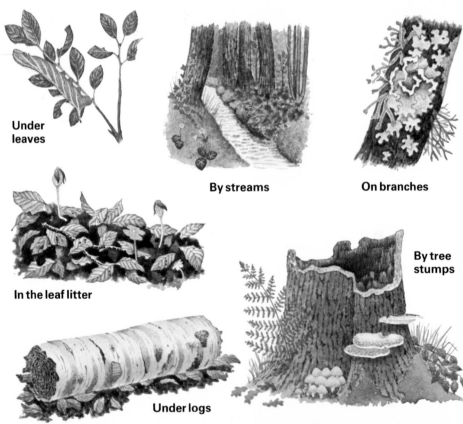

Under leaves

By streams

On branches

In the leaf litter

By tree stumps

Under logs

These are some of the best places to look for wildlife in woodlands. Look in damp, shady places for ferns and mosses, and in clearings for young trees, flowers and insects. Remember to look above you as well as on the ground for animals, and listen for different birds' songs. The sort of trees in your wood will affect the kind of wildlife you find.

Taking care of woodlands

1 Don't pick or damage plants

2 Never start fires

3 Leave nests and animals alone

4 Keep to the paths

5 Take litter home

6 Don't eat anything

A woodland food web

Plants are eaten by many animals which in turn provide food for other animals. This process is known as a "food chain". In this diagram, for example, you can see that plants are eaten by mice and voles which are in turn eaten by Weasels.

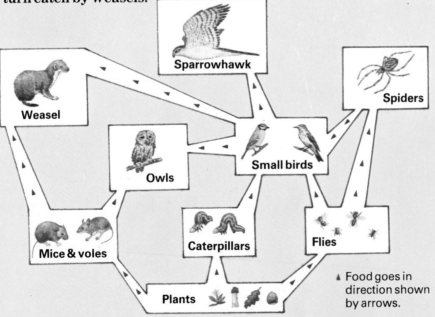

Sparrowhawk

Weasel

Spiders

Owls

Small birds

Mice & voles

Caterpillars

Flies

Plants

▲ Food goes in direction shown by arrows.

Most animals have several kinds of food, so food chains link together to form complex patterns known as "food webs". See if you can follow the food chains that make up the web above. Start with the plants and follow in the direction shown by the arrows. Food webs are delicately balanced and if one plant or animal is removed, every other plant or animal in the web will be affected.

How a wood grows

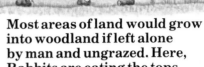

1 Grassland grazed by animals

Most areas of land would grow into woodland if left alone by man and ungrazed. Here, Rabbits are eating the tops of the tree seedlings and stopping them growing.

2 After 7 years without grazing...

On ungrazed land, grasses and other plants grow taller, the climbing plants like Bramble spread, and shrubs like Hawthorn will grow.

3 After 20 years...

Young trees that have been protected under the shrubs start to grow taller. Birch appears first, followed by the slower-growing Oaks and Ashes.

4 After 150 years...

The large woodland trees, such as Oak and Ash, have grown tall, and shade out many of the shrubs and other plants.

Trees

Trees and shrubs are the most important part of a woodland because they live for such a long time, and can therefore provide homes for a large variety of animals. Other plants die away each year, but some trees may live for hundreds of years. When you are in a wood, look out for trees at different stages in their growth – young seedlings pushing up through the leaf litter, saplings with their supple branches, mature trees and very old, twisted ones. Look out for the appearance of flowers and fruits.

Summer and winter

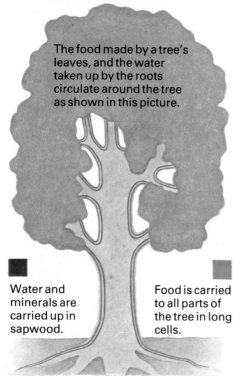

The food made by a tree's leaves, and the water taken up by the roots circulate around the tree as shown in this picture.

Water and minerals are carried up in sapwood.

Food is carried to all parts of the tree in long cells.

Deciduous trees make all their food in summer and lose their leaves in winter. This is because tree roots cannot take up water when the ground is frozen. If the tree still had its leaves in winter, it would lose water through its leaves that it could not replace through its roots. Evergreen trees can keep their leaves in winter because they lose less water through their leaves.

Leaves

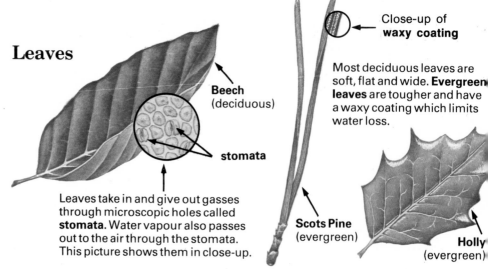

Close-up of **waxy coating**

Beech (deciduous)

stomata

Leaves take in and give out gasses through microscopic holes called **stomata**. Water vapour also passes out to the air through the stomata. This picture shows them in close-up.

Most deciduous leaves are soft, flat and wide. **Evergreen leaves** are tougher and have a waxy coating which limits water loss.

Scots Pine (evergreen)

Holly (evergreen)

Trees that lose all their leaves in autumn are called deciduous, and those which have leaves all the year round are called evergreen. In both types of tree, the leaves contain a green substance called chlorophyll which absorbs sunlight. The leaves use this light energy to make food from water and carbon dioxide (a gas in the air).

The trunk

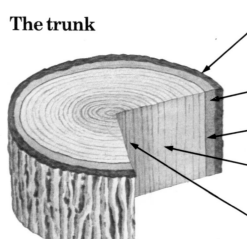

Bark prevents the tree from drying out and protects it from damage by animals and fungi. It also insulates it against very hot or very cold weather.

Long cells under the bark carry food from the leaves to all parts of the tree.

A thin layer, called **cambium,** makes a new layer of sapwood and food cells each year.

The **sapwood** contains tube-like cells which carry sap (water and minerals) from the roots to the rest of the tree.

The **heartwood,** at the centre of the trunk, is made of dead sapwood. It is very hard and makes the tree strong and rigid.

Roots

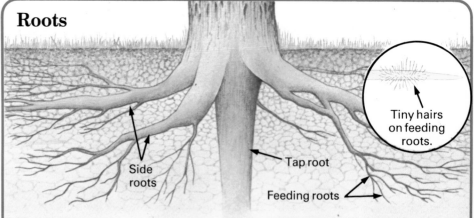

Tiny hairs on feeding roots.

Side roots

Tap root

Feeding roots

Roots support the tree and draw water from the soil. The tap root goes straight into the ground and acts as an anchor for the tree. Side roots also support the tree and usually spread wider than the tree's branches. Smaller feeding roots branch off the main roots; they are covered in tiny hairs and absorb water and minerals.

Broadleaved trees

The English Oak's **male flowers** (catkins) are on same tree as the female flowers.

Seeds and fruits develop from female flowers that have been fertilized by pollen. This **acorn** is a hard fruit, surrounding a single seed.

In autumn, as the **leaves** die, the green chlorophyll breaks down and the leaves change colour.

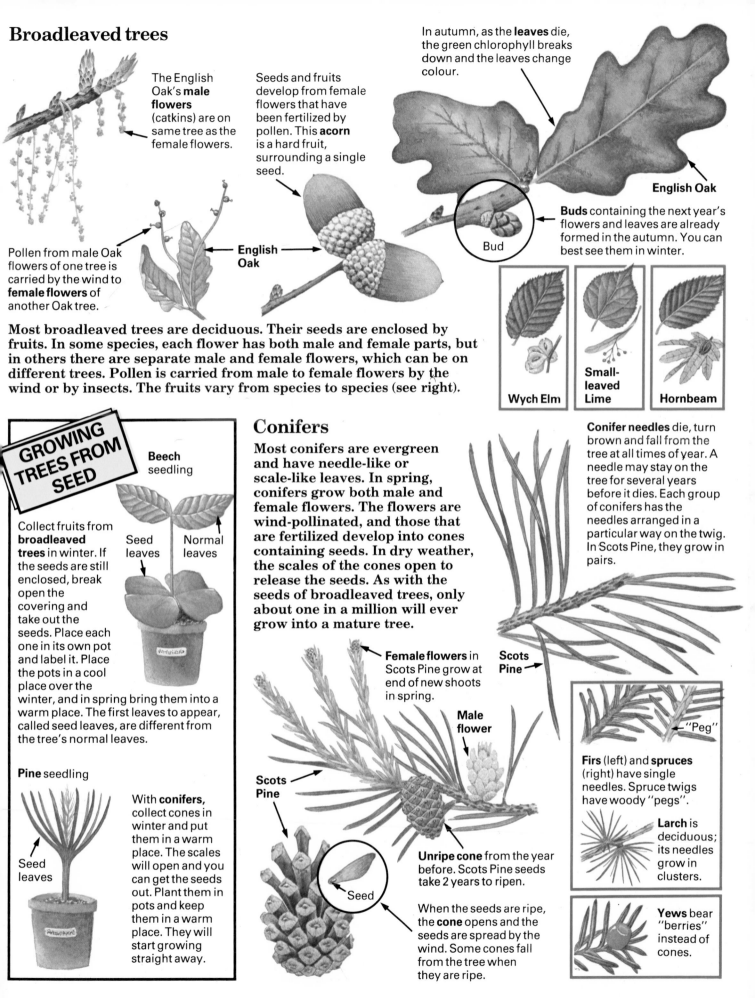

English Oak

Pollen from male Oak flowers of one tree is carried by the wind to **female flowers** of another Oak tree.

English Oak

Buds containing the next year's flowers and leaves are already formed in the autumn. You can best see them in winter.

Bud

Most broadleaved trees are deciduous. Their seeds are enclosed by fruits. In some species, each flower has both male and female parts, but in others there are separate male and female flowers, which can be on different trees. Pollen is carried from male to female flowers by the wind or by insects. The fruits vary from species to species (see right).

Wych Elm

Small-leaved Lime

Hornbeam

GROWING TREES FROM SEED

Beech seedling

Collect fruits from **broadleaved trees** in winter. If the seeds are still enclosed, break open the covering and take out the seeds. Place each one in its own pot and label it. Place the pots in a cool place over the winter, and in spring bring them into a warm place. The first leaves to appear, called seed leaves, are different from the tree's normal leaves.

Seed leaves

Normal leaves

Pine seedling

Seed leaves

With **conifers**, collect cones in winter and put them in a warm place. The scales will open and you can get the seeds out. Plant them in pots and keep them in a warm place. They will start growing straight away.

Conifers

Most conifers are evergreen and have needle-like or scale-like leaves. In spring, conifers grow both male and female flowers. The flowers are wind-pollinated, and those that are fertilized develop into cones containing seeds. In dry weather, the scales of the cones open to release the seeds. As with the seeds of broadleaved trees, only about one in a million will ever grow into a mature tree.

Conifer needles die, turn brown and fall from the tree at all times of year. A needle may stay on the tree for several years before it dies. Each group of conifers has the needles arranged in a particular way on the twig. In Scots Pine, they grow in pairs.

Female flowers in Scots Pine grow at end of new shoots in spring.

Scots Pine

Male flower

Scots Pine

"Peg"

Firs (left) and **spruces** (right) have single needles. Spruce twigs have woody "pegs".

Larch is deciduous; its needles grow in clusters.

Seed

Unripe cone from the year before. Scots Pine seeds take 2 years to ripen.

When the seeds are ripe, the **cone** opens and the seeds are spread by the wind. Some cones fall from the tree when they are ripe.

Yews bear "berries" instead of cones.

Broadleaved woodlands

Britain was once largely covered with broadleaved forests. Man gradually cleared most of them in order to grow crops and graze his animals. The woods that remained were used for hunting and as a source of firewood and building timber. For this reason, most of the broadleaved woods you can see today are not totally natural, and some have even been planted. Trees growing in straight lines are a sign of a plantation.

Woods that have not been much changed by man contain a mixture of trees and shrubs, often with one species more numerous than others. This species is said to be dominant.

A Beech wood

Beech

Holly

Bird's Nest Orchid

Beeches are often found on thin, well-drained soils. Their leaves form such a thick canopy that little light reaches the ground. If the trees are close together, very few other plants can survive. Evergreen shrubs, such as Holly and Yew, can receive light in winter and spring when the Beeches are leafless. Bird's Nest Orchids can live in Beech woods as they feed on dead plants and do not need light to grow.

Layers in woods

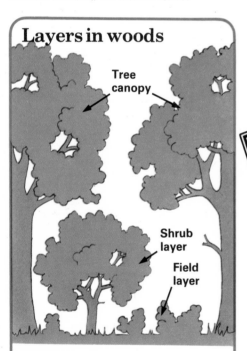

Tree canopy

Shrub layer

Field layer

Plants need light in order to make food. If the tree canopy in a wood lets through enough light, there will be a shrub layer where shrubs and young trees can grow. Below these, there may be a field layer where smaller plants, such as grasses and flowers, grow. Each layer adds to the variety of places in a wood where animals can find food and shelter.

MAN AND WOODS

Most broadleaved woods have at some time been managed by man to produce wood for building, basket-making, fuel, and many other purposes. Some trees were, and still are, coppiced and pollarded. Look for signs that these methods have been used in woods.

Coppicing

1 When trees are coppiced, they are cut down to a stump. Hazel and Sweet Chestnut are often coppiced.

2 Not just one, but several new shoots grow from the cut stump. Several years later, these are cut and used for poles.

3 Old coppiced trees which have not recently been cut have several trunks rather than one.

Pollarding

1 Pollarding means cutting off the tree's branches several feet above the ground. This is done where there are grazing animals, such as deer.

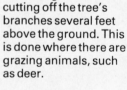

2 The new shoots are too high to be eaten by the grazing animals, so they can grow for several years until they are large enough to be cut.

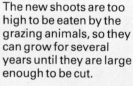

3 A pollarded tree that is left to grow for a long time has several main trunks growing from the point at which it was originally cut.

An Oak wood

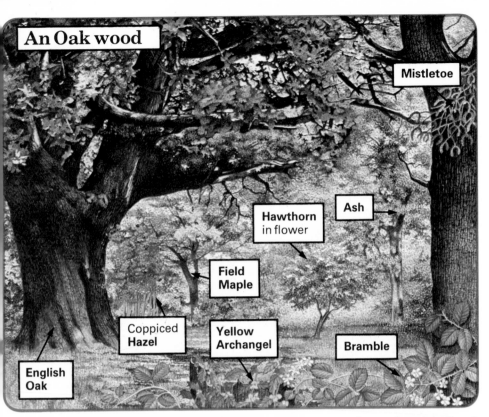

Mistletoe

Ash

Hawthorn in flower

Field Maple

Coppiced Hazel

Yellow Archangel

Bramble

English Oak

In woods where English Oak is dominant, there are often other kinds of trees, such as Ash, Field Maple and Hazel, growing as well. Such woods often do not have a very thick canopy, so many kinds of shrubs and flowers are able to survive. All these different plants together provide a very rich habitat for wildlife. On pages 24-31, there are more pictures of Oak woods, showing the kinds of animals and plants found in them.

An Alder wood

Goat Willow

Alder

Yellow Flag

Alders and Willows grow well on wet ground. Woods of these trees can be good areas for wildlife – especially insects, as there is water as well as the food and shelter provided by the trees.

Flowers in broadleaved woods

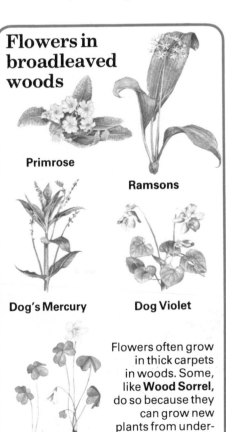

Primrose

Ramsons

Dog's Mercury

Dog Violet

Flowers often grow in thick carpets in woods. Some, like **Wood Sorrel**, do so because they can grow new plants from underground runners.

Shapes of lichens

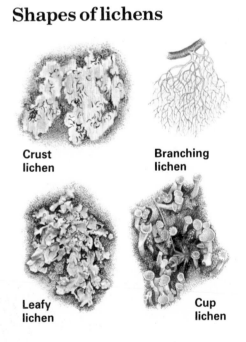

Crust lichen

Branching lichen

Leafy lichen

Cup lichen

Lichens are common in old broadleaved woods, especially on trees with ridged bark, such as Oak and Ash. Lichens are in fact two plants – a microscopic green plant called an alga, and a fungus. They are sensitive to air pollution.

Some broadleaved trees

English Oak

Sessile Oak

Beech

Ash

Alder

Goat Willow

Field Maple

Sycamore

Hazel

Hawthorn

Sweet Chestnut

Dogwood

Coniferous woodlands

Most conifer woods in Britain have been planted for timber. Conifer trees are more often planted than broadleaved trees because they grow faster. Their straight trunks are easy to saw into planks, and their wood is suitable for paper.

Most conifer woods, even natural ones, are rather dark because nearly all conifers are evergreen and grow close together. They often grow in cold areas and in places with poor soil. Despite these difficult conditions, some plants and animals can thrive in coniferous woods. For example, the number of Pine Martens has increased in some plantations.

A Scots Pine wood

Scots Pine

Hairy Birch

Rowan

Juniper

Bilberry

Heather

On poor soils in Scotland and in parts of Northern Europe, there are Scots Pine woods which have not been planted by man. They usually have a canopy of leaves which is less thick than that of other coniferous woods, and often the trees do not grow close together, so there is enough light for other hardy plants, like those shown here, to grow. Trees of several different ages may be found together in the same wood.

Resin

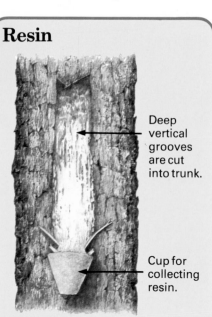

Deep vertical grooves are cut into trunk.

Cup for collecting resin.

The needles, bark and wood of conifers, especially of pines, contain a strong-smelling substance called resin. The bitter taste of resin puts off many animals from feeding on conifers. If a tree is damaged, the sticky resin seals the wound and helps protect the tree from attack by fungi and insects. In some areas resin is collected for the turpentine and chemicals it contains.

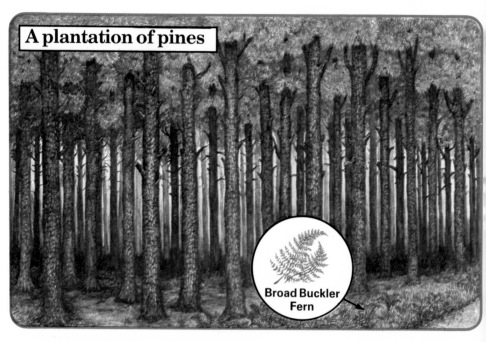

A plantation of pines

Broad Buckler Fern

Trees in plantations are usually in blocks in which all the trees are the same age. They grow close together, and once they are mature, very little light can filter through to the ground until felling starts. This picture shows a block of mature conifers where no plants can grow. Only along the edges of the plantation and along paths can ferns, mosses and a few flowering plants survive.

On mountains

Conifer branches are flexible and can bear a heavy load of snow without breaking.

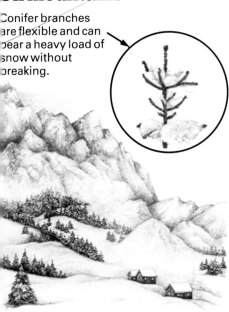

Conifers are often planted on mountains to help stop avalanches. They can survive much better than most broadleaved trees in very cold weather. Snow helps protect them from severe frost.

On sand

Maritime Pines come from the hot, dry Mediterranean area but can be grown on sand dunes in colder areas.

Maritime Pine

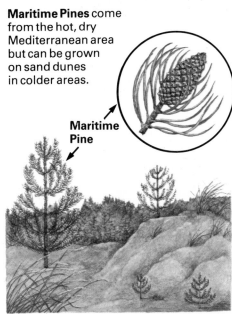

Conifers, especially pines, need less water than broadleaved trees and can grow in dry, sandy soils. Some, like Maritime Pines, are planted on sand dunes, where they help stop sand blowing away.

Looking at cones

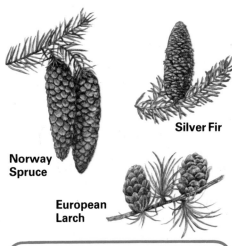

Norway Spruce

Silver Fir

European Larch

North American conifers

Sitka Spruce

Lodgepole Pine

Douglas Fir

These trees have been introduced from North America and are grown in Europe for timber.

Plants of a Scots Pine wood

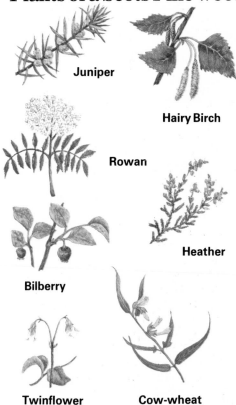

Juniper

Hairy Birch

Rowan

Heather

Bilberry

Twinflower

Cow-wheat

Plantations and wildlife

Some insects, birds and mammals benefit from plantations, but many cannot live there because there is no food or shelter for them. Here are some of the ways in which more wildlife can be encouraged to live in a plantation:

Planting some broadleaved trees amongst or alongside conifers allows birds and other animals that depend on broadleaved trees to live in a plantation.

Ponds or streams in plantations, if they are not too close to the conifers, will contain water plants and insects, which will in turn attract other animals.

A few old trees and dead logs left in a plantation will provide nesting sites for birds, food for insects and fungi, and shelter for many creatures. Bats, for example, may roost in hollow trees.

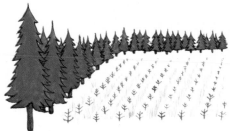

Planting a block of young trees next to older ones helps provide a variety of layers in a plantation. This variety increases the number of different kinds of animals that can live there.

Plants in woodlands

The sheltered damp climate inside a wood helps to protect the plants from drought, frosts and strong winds. But the lack of light under the trees makes it difficult for some plants to survive. Try comparing the numbers and kinds of plants in the dark part of a wood with those in a lighter part.

The kinds of plant that grow in a wood also depend a lot on the soils and climate of the area. For example, Wood Sorrel is often found on poor, thin soils; Dog's Mercury usually grows on richer soil, and ferns and mosses grow best in wetter areas.

Plants in the shade

Some plants, like **Holly,** stay green all year round. In deciduous woods they use some of the light that reaches them in winter and spring when other trees have no leaves.

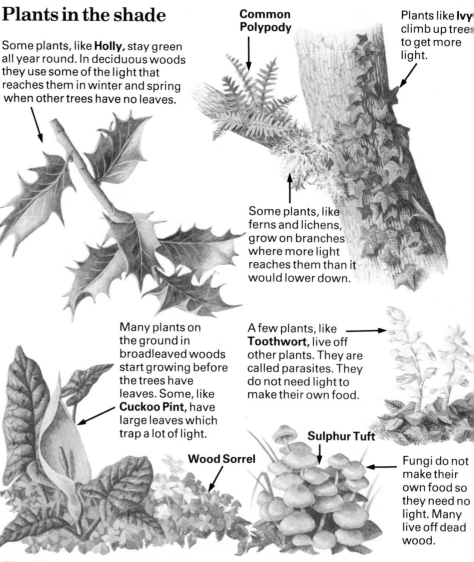

Common Polypody

Plants like **Ivy** climb up trees to get more light.

Some plants, like ferns and lichens, grow on branches where more light reaches them than it would lower down.

Many plants on the ground in broadleaved woods start growing before the trees have leaves. Some, like **Cuckoo Pint,** have large leaves which trap a lot of light.

A few plants, like **Toothwort,** live off other plants. They are called parasites. They do not need light to make their own food.

Sulphur Tuft

Wood Sorrel

Fungi do not make their own food so they need no light. Many live off dead wood.

The plants shown above all have different ways of surviving in the shade. Their leaves are often larger than when they grow in the open, so that they can trap as much light as possible. Plants that do not make their own food are not usually green as they contain no chlorophyll.

An early start

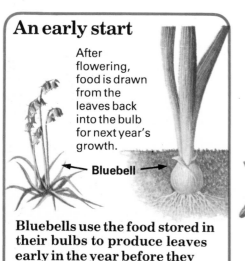

After flowering, food is drawn from the leaves back into the bulb for next year's growth.

Bluebell

Bluebells use the food stored in their bulbs to produce leaves early in the year before they are shaded by the trees.

LOOKING AT FERNS

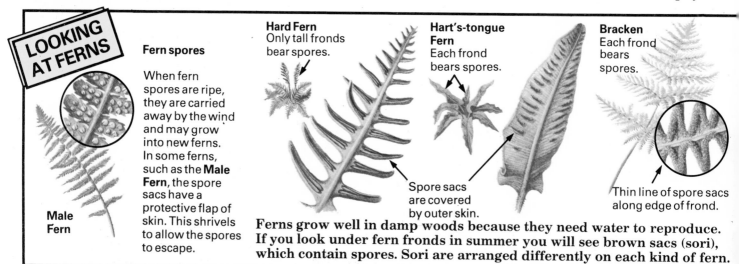

Fern spores

When fern spores are ripe, they are carried away by the wind and may grow into new ferns. In some ferns, such as the **Male Fern,** the spore sacs have a protective flap of skin. This shrivels to allow the spores to escape.

Male Fern

Hard Fern
Only tall fronds bear spores.

Hart's-tongue Fern
Each frond bears spores.

Bracken
Each frond bears spores.

Spore sacs are covered by outer skin.

Thin line of spore sacs along edge of frond.

Ferns grow well in damp woods because they need water to reproduce. If you look under fern fronds in summer you will see brown sacs (sori), which contain spores. Sori are arranged differently on each kind of fern.

Fungi

DO NOT TASTE FUNGI WITHOUT EXPERT ADVICE. SOME ARE POISONOUS.

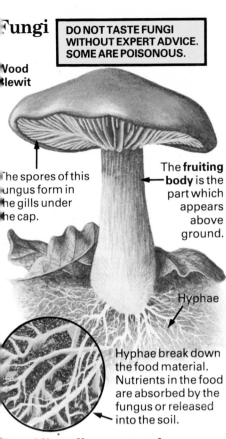

Wood Blewit

The spores of this fungus form in the gills under the cap.

The **fruiting body** is the part which appears above ground.

Hyphae

Hyphae break down the food material. Nutrients in the food are absorbed by the fungus or released into the soil.

Fungi live all year round as a mass of threads, called hyphae, buried in the material on which they feed. Once a year, often in autumn, fruiting bodies are formed. These contain the spores from which new fungi can grow.

Shapes of fungi

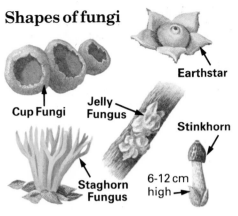

Earthstar

Cup Fungi

Jelly Fungus

Stinkhorn

Staghorn Fungus

6-12 cm high

Not all fungi have a mushroom-like fruiting body. Here you can see some unusual ones.

Orchids and fungi

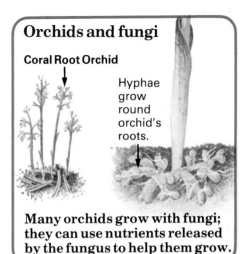

Coral Root Orchid

Hyphae grow round orchid's roots.

Many orchids grow with fungi; they can use nutrients released by the fungus to help them grow.

Helping and harming trees

Some fungi live off growing plants instead of dead ones. This can either harm or help the plant. Fly Agaric and Silver Birch help each other but Birch Polypore will kill the tree.

Birch Polypore feeds on the tree but the tree gets nothing in return.

Silver Birch

Fly Agaric obtains sugars from the tree but provides it with nutrients that the tree cannot get easily from the soil.

Plants in the light

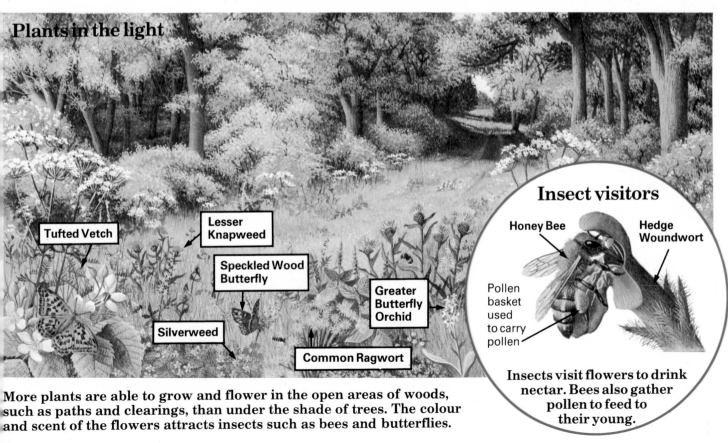

Tufted Vetch

Lesser Knapweed

Speckled Wood Butterfly

Silverweed

Greater Butterfly Orchid

Common Ragwort

Insect visitors

Honey Bee

Hedge Woundwort

Pollen basket used to carry pollen

Insects visit flowers to drink nectar. Bees also gather pollen to feed to their young.

More plants are able to grow and flower in the open areas of woods, such as paths and clearings, than under the shade of trees. The colour and scent of the flowers attracts insects such as bees and butterflies.

Insects

Trees that have grown naturally in Europe since the last Ice Age, such as some oaks, may have hundreds of species of insects living on them. But there are fewer on trees that have been introduced here from other parts of the world, such as some of the planted conifers. The insects normally associated with these trees get left behind in their native countries, and European insects may not be able to adapt to the new trees.

Some insects feed on several species of trees, but some have only one food plant. For example, caterpillars of the Purple Emperor Butterfly eat only Willow leaves.

Life cycle

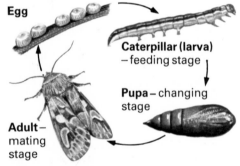

Egg

Caterpillar (larva) – feeding stage

Pupa – changing stage

Adult – mating stage

Many insects, like this moth, go through four stages in their lives. Others – Greenfly, for example – hatch out looking like tiny adults.

Feeding in trees and shrubs

On wood...
Some larvae, like this **Goat Moth caterpillar,** tunnel into trees and feed on the wood.

Purple Emperor Butterflies

On sap...
Butterflies and moths often feed on the sugary sap that runs from damaged trees.

Aphids, such as **Greenfly,** use their sharp mouthparts to pierce plant veins and suck up the sap. They pass out unwanted sap as drops of sticky "honeydew".

Honeydew

On leaves...
Caterpillars, like these **Sawfly larvae,** may completely strip a tree of its leaves. They eat the soft parts first.

Inside leaves...
The larvae of some insects, such as flies and moths, make tunnels or "mines" inside leaves as they feed.

Bramble leaf mine

Holly leaf mine

On honeydew...
Bees, ants and butterflies often feed on honeydew, which may form a sticky coating on leaves.

Purple Hairstreak

Trees offer a variety of food for a huge number of insect species. Adult insects often lay their eggs on the food plant so that the larvae will be next to their food when they hatch. The larvae spend most of their time eating, as this is the stage in their lives when they grow.

A parasite

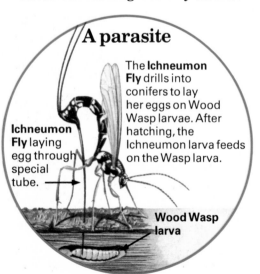

The **Ichneumon Fly** drills into conifers to lay her eggs on Wood Wasp larvae. After hatching, the Ichneumon larva feeds on the Wasp larva.

Ichneumon Fly laying egg through special tube.

Wood Wasp larva

An insect hunter

Large muscles for powerful flight.

Robber Fly

Strong bristles to trap insects.

The Robber Fly hunts flying insects. It grips its prey with its powerful legs and sucks the insect's body dry.

Money Spiders

Spiders are not insects.

Money Spiders spin hammock-like webs to trap insects. They bundle their prey in silk to stop them from escaping.

Different types of galls

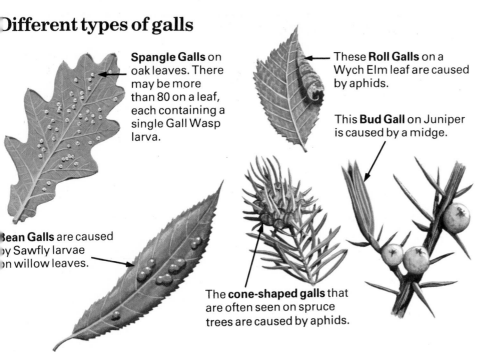

Spangle Galls on oak leaves. There may be more than 80 on a leaf, each containing a single Gall Wasp larva.

These **Roll Galls** on a Wych Elm leaf are caused by aphids.

This **Bud Gall** on Juniper is caused by a midge.

Bean Galls are caused by Sawfly larvae on willow leaves.

The **cone-shaped galls** that are often seen on spruce trees are caused by aphids.

On many trees and shrubs, particularly oaks and willows, you may find growths like the ones shown here. They are called galls, and are produced by the tree in reaction to irritation caused by an insect egg or larva. The insect grows inside the gall, where it has plenty of food and is well protected. Some insects live singly in galls – others in groups.

Oak Marble Galls

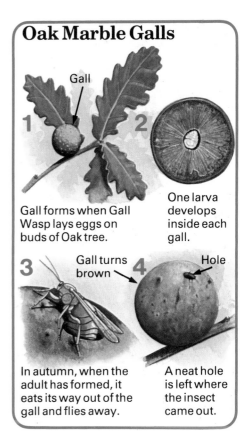

Gall

1 Gall forms when Gall Wasp lays eggs on buds of Oak tree.

2 One larva develops inside each gall.

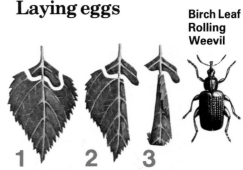

3 Gall turns brown

In autumn, when the adult has formed, it eats its way out of the gall and flies away.

4 Hole

A neat hole is left where the insect came out.

Disguise

Bud

Caterpillars of **Purple Hairstreak Butterfly** look like oak buds.

Caterpillars of **Great Oak Beauty Moth** look like oak twigs.

Angle Shades Moths look like dead leaves.

Merveille du Jour Moths look like tree lichens.

Pupa of **Black Hairstreak Butterfly** looks like a bird dropping.

Some insects protect themselves from enemies by looking like their surroundings; other insects mimic things their enemies will not eat.

Protection

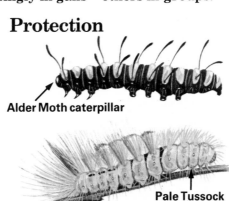

Alder Moth caterpillar

Pale Tussock Moth caterpillar

Birds and other animals learn to leave brightly coloured or hairy caterpillars alone, as they are often poisonous or hard to eat.

Defence

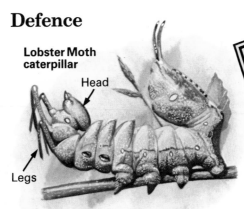

Lobster Moth caterpillar

Head

Legs

This caterpillar holds its head back and waves its legs about if it sees an enemy. It may also squirt formic acid to drive them away.

Laying eggs

Birch Leaf Rolling Weevil

1 **2** **3**

This weevil rolls up a leaf to lay its eggs in. First it cuts the leaf in two places. Then it rolls the leaf into a tube with its legs. Finally it turns over the leaf tip to seal the tube with the eggs inside.

LOOKING FOR INSECTS

If you shake tree branches like this, many insects will fall onto the white cloth.

The woodland floor

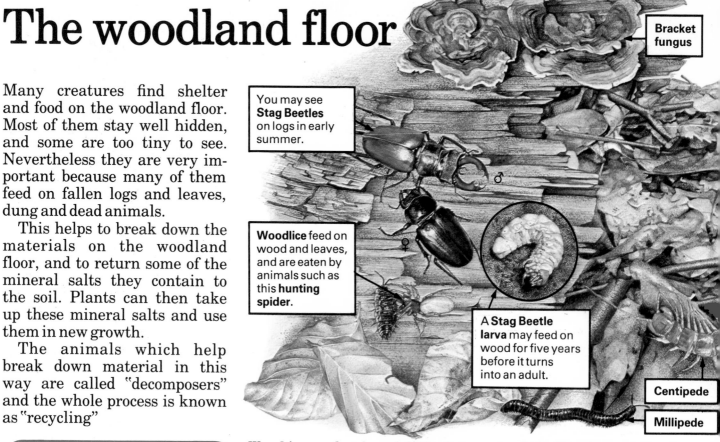

Bracket fungus

You may see **Stag Beetles** on logs in early summer.

Woodlice feed on wood and leaves, and are eaten by animals such as this **hunting spider**.

A **Stag Beetle larva** may feed on wood for five years before it turns into an adult.

Centipede

Millipede

Many creatures find shelter and food on the woodland floor. Most of them stay well hidden, and some are too tiny to see. Nevertheless they are very important because many of them feed on fallen logs and leaves, dung and dead animals.

This helps to break down the materials on the woodland floor, and to return some of the mineral salts they contain to the soil. Plants can then take up these mineral salts and use them in new growth.

The animals which help break down material in this way are called "decomposers" and the whole process is known as "recycling"

Dor beetles

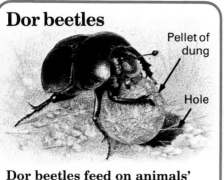

Pellet of dung

Hole

Dor beetles feed on animals' dung. They also bury pellets of dung and lay their eggs on them. When the larvae hatch, they feed on the pellets.

Burying beetles

Dead **Blue Tit**

Burying beetles feed on dead animals and lay their eggs near the corpses. To keep off other insects such as Bluebottles, they bury the corpse by digging out the soil under it.

Wood is very hard, and difficult for animals to digest, so a fallen log takes several years to break down completely. At first, bark beetles and fungi get under the bark; then, when the bark has been loosened, other insects bore into the log, allowing bacteria and more fungi to work their way inside. As the wood gets softer, more wood-eating beetle larvae burrow into the log to feed. Eventually, the log crumbles into the litter.

Bark beetles

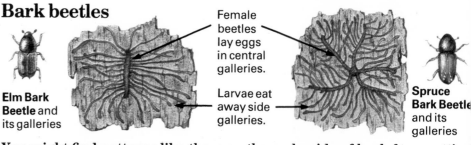

Female beetles lay eggs in central galleries.

Elm Bark Beetle and its galleries

Larvae eat away side galleries.

Spruce Bark Beetle and its galleries

You might find patterns like these on the underside of bark from rotting trees. They are made by different kinds of bark beetles which bore into bark, then make tunnels called "galleries" in which to lay their eggs. When the larvae hatch, they eat away side galleries and pupate in them.

LOOKING AT LEAF LITTER

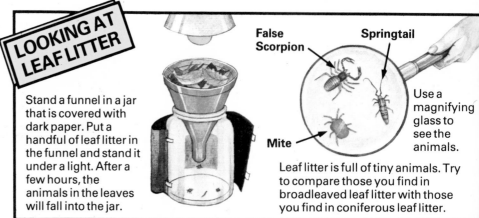

False Scorpion

Springtail

Mite

Use a magnifying glass to see the animals.

Stand a funnel in a jar that is covered with dark paper. Put a handful of leaf litter in the funnel and stand it under a light. After a few hours, the animals in the leaves will fall into the jar.

Leaf litter is full of tiny animals. Try to compare those you find in broadleaved leaf litter with those you find in coniferous leaf litter.

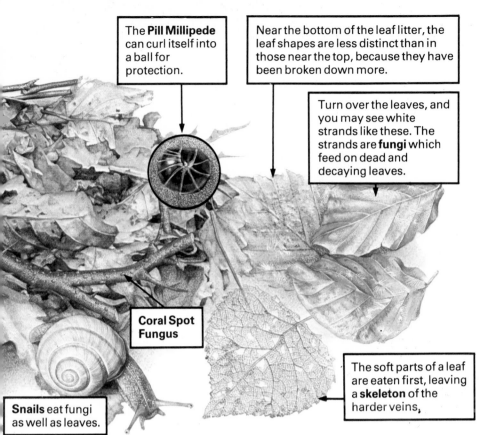

The **Pill Millipede** can curl itself into a ball for protection.

Near the bottom of the leaf litter, the leaf shapes are less distinct than in those near the top, because they have been broken down more.

Turn over the leaves, and you may see white strands like these. The strands are **fungi** which feed on dead and decaying leaves.

Coral Spot Fungus

The soft parts of a leaf are eaten first, leaving a **skeleton** of the harder veins.

Snails eat fungi as well as leaves.

In deciduous woods, the leaves fall to earth in autumn, but by the following spring or summer (depending on the type of leaf), they have usually all gone. This is because large decomposers, such as millipedes, earwigs, slugs and snails break up the leaves as they eat them. Some of these creatures in turn provide food for meat-eaters, like centipedes. Fungi and bacteria are also important in breaking down dead leaves.

Conifer woods

Sickener toadstool

Pine needles

In conifer woods, the floor is often covered in a deep bed of needles. This is because not many animals can digest the tough needles and there are few large decomposers, like Earthworms, to mix the needles into the soil. However, many fungi can break down the needles and help in recycling nutrients.

Earthworms

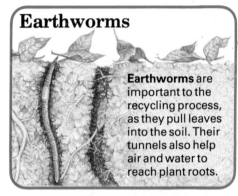

Earthworms are important to the recycling process, as they pull leaves into the soil. Their tunnels also help air and water to reach plant roots.

Wood Ants

1

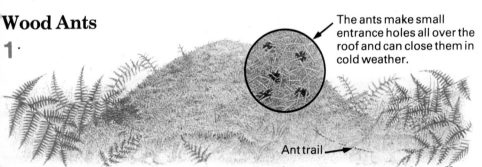

The ants make small entrance holes all over the roof and can close them in cold weather.

Ant trail

In some woods, you may see a large mound of twigs, stems and needles, like the one shown above. This is made by Wood Ants to cover and protect their nest, which is mainly underground.

3

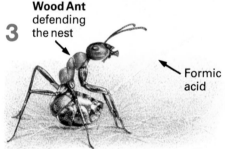

Wood Ant defending the nest

Formic acid

Wood Ants can curl their bodies forward and squirt formic acid at their enemies to sting them.

2 Inside the nest, there are thousands of tunnels and chambers.

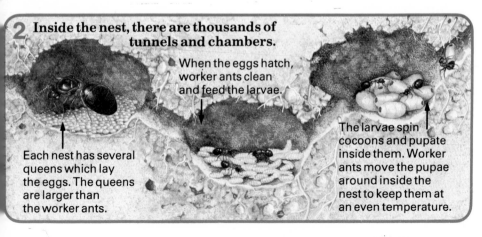

When the eggs hatch, worker ants clean and feed the larvae.

Each nest has several queens which lay the eggs. The queens are larger than the worker ants.

The larvae spin cocoons and pupate inside them. Worker ants move the pupae around inside the nest to keep them at an even temperature.

4

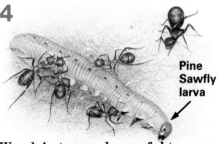

Pine Sawfly larva

Wood Ants may be useful to man because they eat many insects which are harmful to trees. The ants can carry prey that is much larger than themselves.

Birds

A variety of birds live in woodlands because there is plenty of food and many safe places to nest. The birds can also shelter from bad weather and hide from their enemies.

Many of the birds you see in a woodland will be searching for food under leaves, tree bark or in the leaf litter. Parent birds may make hundreds of trips each day to collect food for their young.

A bird's beak may give you a clue to what it feeds on. For instance, seed-eaters have short, strong beaks for crushing seeds and birds of prey have sharp, hooked beaks for tearing flesh. How many kinds of beak can you find on these two pages?

Feeding layers

Oak wood

Blue Tit
Wood Warbler
Spotted Flycatcher
Nightingale
Wren
Blackbird

Treecreeper
Woodpecker
Nuthatch
Woodcock

Scots Pine wood

Siskin
Goldcrest
Crested Tit
Wood Pigeon
Capercaillie

Birds are able to fly and climb to reach food in all the woodland layers. Many birds can feed close together because each kind of bird stays mainly in one layer to look for food.

Territory

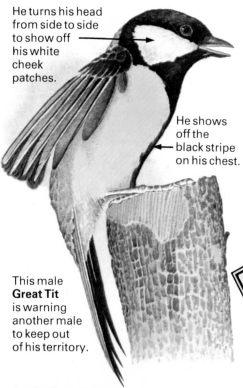

He turns his head from side to side to show off his white cheek patches.

He shows off the black stripe on his chest.

This male **Great Tit** is warning another male to keep out of his territory.

In the breeding season, most woodland birds claim a small area of woodland as their own territory. They use this area to feed and nest in. The male birds defend their territory by special songs and threat displays.

Song

Wood Warbler

Most woodland birds have loud, clear songs to communicate with each other in dense undergrowth.

Colour

Male Chaffinch

Female Chaffinch

Male birds are often more colourful than females. They show off their bright colours to attract a mate.

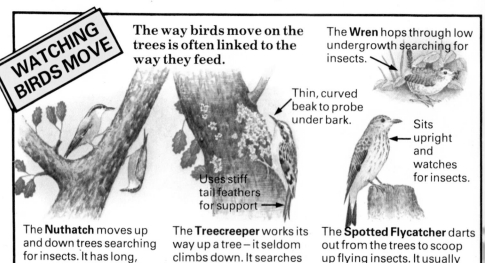

WATCHING BIRDS MOVE

The way birds move on the trees is often linked to the way they feed.

The **Wren** hops through low undergrowth searching for insects.

Thin, curved beak to probe under bark.

Uses stiff tail feathers for support

Sits upright and watches for insects.

The **Nuthatch** moves up and down trees searching for insects. It has long, curved claws for climbing.

The **Treecreeper** works its way up a tree – it seldom climbs down. It searches under the bark for insects.

The **Spotted Flycatcher** darts out from the trees to scoop up flying insects. It usually goes back to its perch.

Nests on branches

Lining of feathers helps to keep young birds warm.

The **Goldcrest's** nest is made of moss, hair, feathers and spiders' webs.

Many woodland birds build their nests high in the trees where the eggs and young will be hidden from enemies such as Squirrels and Weasels. The Goldcrest often hangs its tiny nest at the end of a branch.

A woodland hunter

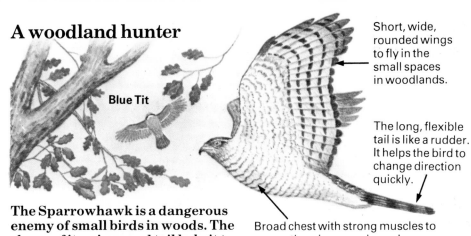

Blue Tit

Short, wide, rounded wings to fly in the small spaces in woodlands.

The long, flexible tail is like a rudder. It helps the bird to change direction quickly.

Broad chest with strong muscles to power the wings on a long chase.

The Sparrowhawk is a dangerous enemy of small birds in woods. The shape of its wings and tail help it to twist and turn quickly as it hunts.

Opening nuts

The Nuthatch wedges nuts in tree trunks and hammers them open with its sharp beak.

Woodpeckers

Long, sticky tongue to lick out insects.

Long, curved claws to help the bird cling to tree trunks.

Strong, stiff tail feathers for support

Great Spotted Woodpecker

Woodpeckers chisel into decaying tree trunks to search for insects. You may see trees in a wood covered with the holes they make.

Nests in holes

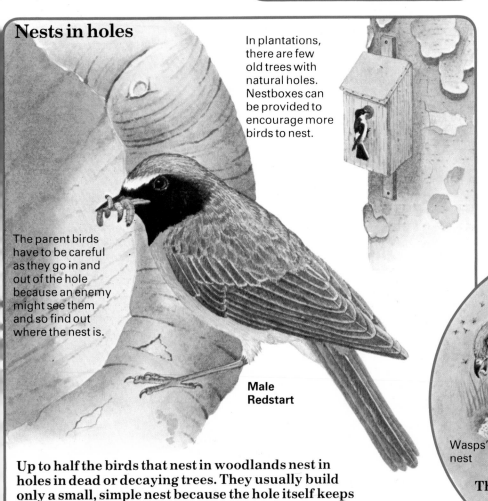

In plantations, there are few old trees with natural holes. Nestboxes can be provided to encourage more birds to nest.

The parent birds have to be careful as they go in and out of the hole because an enemy might see them and so find out where the nest is.

Male Redstart

Up to half the birds that nest in woodlands nest in holes in dead or decaying trees. They usually build only a small, simple nest because the hole itself keeps the eggs and young warm and hidden from enemies.

Special diets

Wasps' nest

The Honey Buzzard uses its blunt claws to dig into wasps' nests. It eats the grubs inside.

Mammals

Mammals are warm-blooded animals (they can maintain an even body temperature); nearly all of them give birth to live young, which feed on their mother's milk; most of them are covered in hair or fur.

Most mammals are active only at night (see next page) or are well hidden in the undergrowth, but if you look carefully you will find signs that mammals are there. Look for food remains, droppings, pathways and burrows; these will help you to picture how the animals live and feed. Listen for squeaks and rustling noises made by small mammals, and look for tracks in mud or snow.

Many woodland mammals are plant-eaters and some may cause a lot of damage in plantations. Most of the large meat-eating mammals, such as Wolves, are extinct in Britain because of hunting by man.

Escaping from danger

Grey Squirrel

Colour of coat makes it hard to see against tree bark.

It keeps the trunk between itself and the danger, and may flick its tail to warn other squirrels.

Squirrels cannot defend themselves very easily. If they are on the ground when they see danger, such as a Fox, they climb a tree.

Food

Look for food remains under trees.

Red Squirrels collect pine cones and bite off the scales one by one, licking out the seeds. You may hear them eating.

How antlers grow

These knobs are called pedicles. They are on top of bones in the head.

Red Deer

1
Male deer grow a new set of antlers each year. In Red Deer, they start to show in the spring a few weeks after the old antlers are shed.

Velvet can be easily damaged if the deer knocks its antlers.

2
The growing antlers are covered in a soft skin called velvet. Tiny blood vessels under the velvet carry food and minerals to the antlers.

The velvet dries up and peels off in strips.

3
Just before the breeding season in September or October, the blood supply to the antlers is cut off and they stop growing.

Deer get rid of the old velvet by rubbing the antlers against small trees or springy bushes.

Blood stains where velvet has been rubbed off.

4
After the breeding season, the antlers are no longer needed. They are "cast" (drop off) one at a time between February and April.

Using antlers

In the breeding season (called the "rut"), Red Deer fight with their antlers to win a herd of females for mating. They lock antlers and push against each other until one gives way. This test of strength makes sure that the fittest and strongest deer will mate.

Eating antlers

Wood Mouse

Tooth marks show up as fine lines.

Antlers contain minerals such as calcium, and may be gnawed by deer or even by small animals.

Climbing trees

Bank Voles will eat the bark of both conifers and broadleaved trees.

Hazel catkins

The **Bank Vole's** long toes help it to grip the branches as it climbs.

In winter, when other food is hard to find, many mammals feed on tree bark. Bank Voles may climb up into the trees to feed. They gnaw off the thick outer layer of bark and feed on the living layer beneath.

Nosing out food

Wild Boars are not found in Britain.

The Wild Boar has a long, sensitive nose which it uses to search for roots, bulbs, fungi and small animals on the woodland floor.

SIGNS ON BARK

Look for these feeding signs on tree bark.

Squirrel

Often feeds high in trees. The gnawed bark peels off in strips.

Bank Vole

Feeds on trunk and branches. Look for teeth marks and pieces of gnawed bark on ground.

Deer

Strips large pieces of bark upwards. Also rubs antlers on trees.

Weasels

Weasels nest in tree holes, under stones or logs, or even in mice or vole burrows. Male Weasels defend a territory around their home.

These four-week-old Weasels eat the meat their parents catch for them. By the time they are eight weeks old they can hunt alone.

Weasels feed mainly on small mammals such as mice and voles, but will also rob birds' nests. The Weasel's small, thin body (only 20cm long) allows it to squeeze into the burrows of its prey.

Weasels kill their prey, such as this **Wood Mouse**, by biting it in the neck.

Animals at night

Many woodland animals rest during the day and become active at night. However, several of these "nocturnal" animals tend to move around and feed mainly at dusk or at dawn, rather than all through the night. Some of them can see much better than we can in the dark, while others rely on their acute sense of smell or hearing.

· Before you go watching animals in a wood at night, it is a good idea to get to know the area well in the daytime. Wear dark clothes so that you are more difficult for the animals to see, and dress warmly.

How owls hunt

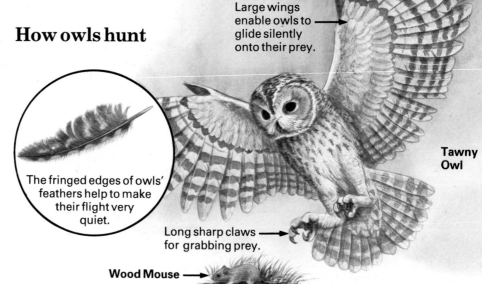

Large wings enable owls to glide silently onto their prey.

The fringed edges of owls' feathers help to make their flight very quiet.

Tawny Owl

Long sharp claws for grabbing prey.

Wood Mouse →

Owls hunt at night for animals such as mice, voles, worms and beetles. They can see well in the dark and their hearing is extremely good. Their flight is almost totally silent.

How bats hunt

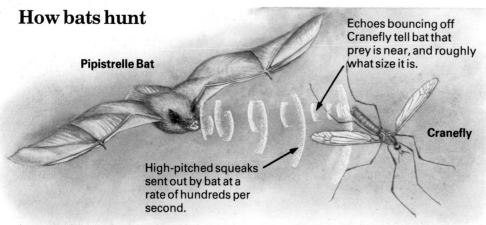

Pipistrelle Bat

Echoes bouncing off Cranefly tell bat that prey is near, and roughly what size it is.

Cranefly

High-pitched squeaks sent out by bat at a rate of hundreds per second.

Bats find insects at night by sending out high-pitched noises and picking up echoes with their sensitive ears. The echoes tell them the position of nearby objects, and whether or not they are moving. We cannot hear these noises, but we can hear alarm signals made by bats.

Dormouse

Long, thin toes grip branches. Tail helps it keep balance.

Dormice climb among branches at night in search of food. They often eat Hazelnuts in autumn.

Badger-watching

Badgers usually come out as it is getting dark. Each **sett** may have several exits.

Look for a heap of **old bedding material** and **soil** dug out of the sett.

Stand near a tree or some bushes, and keep as still and quiet as possible.

There may be a **dung pit** nearby with fresh droppings in it.

Well-trodden **paths** leading from sett.

The signs shown in this picture will tell you if a sett is in use or not. Approach the area before dusk, with the wind blowing in your face. Badgers have a strong sense of smell and will not appear if they detect humans.

Tree trunks at night

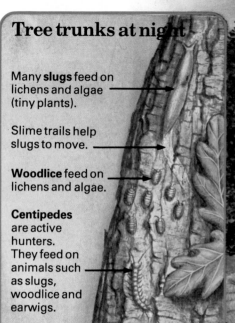

Many **slugs** feed on lichens and algae (tiny plants).

Slime trails help slugs to move.

Woodlice feed on lichens and algae.

Centipedes are active hunters. They feed on animals such as slugs, woodlice and earwigs.

Many small animals lose water easily, so they come out at night when the air is cool and damp. They often climb trees in search of food.

Attracting a mate

1 Moths

Many moths look for a mate at night. The female releases scent to attract a male and waits for the male to find her. Her scent may be carried over long distances. The moths shown here are Black Arches Moths.

The **male moth** has tiny hairs on the branches of his antennae which catch the scent. He follows the scent until he finds the female.

Female moth

Antenna

COUNTING WOODLICE

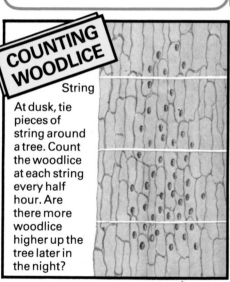

String

At dusk, tie pieces of string around a tree. Count the woodlice at each string every half hour. Are there more woodlice higher up the tree later in the night?

2 Fox

On spring nights, you may hear the long, eerie scream of a vixen calling her mate. The dog Fox may bark in reply.

3 Oak Bush Cricket

The male sits in oak trees at night and drums his hind leg on a leaf to attract a female for mating.

Eyes at night

Special layer at back of eyes looks red in torch-light.

Badger

Many animals have a special layer in their eyes to help them see in the dark.

4 Woodcock

At dusk in spring, male Woodcocks perform their display flight, known as "roding". They make grunts and sharp cries and then listen for the gentle whistling noises made by the females, who call them down to mate.

Spring

Broadleaved Woods

The wood begins to come to life in spring. As the trees come into leaf, caterpillars hatch out and feed on the soft new leaves. Other insects and a few mammals, such as bats, come out of hibernation and migrant birds arrive to nest in the wood.

Birds spend a lot of time singing to attract a mate or defend a territory. Mammal young are usually born in early spring so they will have time to mature before the next winter.

Migration

Chiffchaffs migrate at night.

In spring, many birds travel from their winter feeding grounds in Africa to woods in Europe. These regular journeys are called migration and the birds are called migrants.

Deciduous tree flowers

Beech flowers in April or May.

Female

Male

Ash flowers in April.

Male

Female

Female

Silver Birch flowers in April.

Male

Many deciduous tree flowers open before the leaves. While the twigs are bare there is more chance of the pollen being blown by the wind from male to female flowers.

An Oak wood in spring

Jays build their nests of dead twigs. The female lays about six eggs in April or May.

Young **Grey Squirrels** are born in the nest (the drey) in early spring.

The male **Blue Tit** often feeds caterpillars to his mate during courtship.

The male **Roe Deer** leaves his scent on vegetation to mark off an area of the wood as his territory.

Soft, bright green leaves start to come out of the buds on the **Hazel** twigs.

The **Hedgehog** wakes up from hibernation and begins to search for insects and worms in the leaf litter.

The female **Woodcock** is difficult to see when she is sitting on her eggs. This makes it hard for enemies to find the nest.

The caterpillar of the **White Admiral Butterfly** wakes up from hibernation and feeds on **Honeysuckle** leaves.

Dog Violet

Most **woodland plants** grow and flower in spring before they are shaded by the trees.

Wood Anemone

Celandine

APRIL 4TH
Saw a Robin singing in an Oak tree. Another Robin nearby.

New Bracken fronds unfolding

Counted 12 Rooks' nests

2 kinds of flowers
male
female

Dog's Mercury

Moss growing near stream

It is a good idea to keep a diary of how your wood changes over the year. Make notes and sketches like these in a notebook.

Ivy berries are ripe in early spring. Birds may eat them and help to scatter the seeds.

Bumble Bees in spring

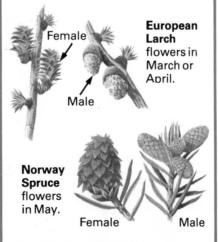

Male **Goat Willow** catkins

Queen Bee drinking nectar

The queen wakes up and flies around to find a place to build a nest and lay her eggs.

Coniferous Woods

In a conifer wood in spring, the trees shade the ground almost as much as they do in summer. There are few plants flowering on the woodland floor. But, as in a broadleaved wood, the trees flower and grow new leaves — look out for pale green shoots at the end of the branches. Insects hatch out to feed on the new needles and migrant birds, return to the wood to nest.

Capercaillies

Male

Female

In spring, male Capercaillies perform this special display to defend their territory and attract a mate. They jump into the air and clap their wings.

Coniferous tree flowers

Female

European Larch flowers in March or April.

Male

Norway Spruce flowers in May.

Female

Male

Conifer tree flowers open at about the same time as the new needles grow in spring.

A Pine wood in spring

The female **Crossbill** sits on her eggs for about two weeks. The male feeds her.

Scots Pine tree

Pine Martens have about three young in March or April. They stay in the nest, while their mother goes out to feed.

Juniper bushes flower from May to June.

Bilberry bushes flower from April to June.

Pinewood plants grow new leaves and build up stores of food.

Tormentil

Lesser Twayblade

Chickweed Wintergreen

Summer

Broadleaved Woods

The thick canopy of leaves on the trees and shrubs in summer provides shelter and protection for nesting birds and young mammals.

Some small birds that hatched out in spring have left the nest already. Their parents may have another family during the summer.

You will see many flying insects in the wood in summer. They are an important source of food for Bats and birds, like Flycatchers, that have families to feed.

Growing up

Fox cubs often play outside their home. This helps to develop their muscles and they learn how to use their senses.

Feeding the young

The female tears up food caught by the male and feeds the young for about three weeks after they hatch.

Sparrowhawk young hatch out in early summer when their parents can catch many young birds to feed them.

An Oak wood in summer

Blue Tits feed their young mainly on caterpillars. The young grow their feathers by the end of June.

Jays feed their young on insects, worms and small animals. They may also steal eggs and young from other birds.

Young **Grey Squirrels** explore their surroundings and watch their mother to find out what to eat.

Roe Deer fawns are born in May or June. Their spotted coat helps to hide them from enemies in the woodland shadows.

The female **Woodcock** may carry her young to safety if the nest is disturbed.

Hazel leaves are fully open and make food for the tree. Fruits start to form towards the tips of the shoots.

When young **Hedgehogs** are three weeks old, they start to leave the nest and follow their mother as she looks for food.

White Admiral Butterflies emerge from the pupa in early summer. They find a mate and the female lays her eggs before the end of summer.

Honeysuckle

Fruits form on the **flowering plants** and the leaves die back. **Celandine** may lose all its leaves by summer.

Wood Anemone

Dog Violet

JULY 11TH

Saw a Flycatcher on edge of wood — hovering to catch insects.

Fern leaves are fully out

Fritillary Butterflies were feeding on Bramble in clearing

Try keeping separate areas for birds, trees, flowers and insects. You could also put the date at the top of each page.

Ivy grows new leaves in summer.

Bumble Bees in summer

Worker **Bumble Bees** hatching out.

"Honey pot" of nectar

The eggs hatch into workers, drones (males), and new queens. The drones and new queens mate.

Coniferous Woods

Summer is the busiest season of the year in a conifer wood. The plants on the woodland floor are in flower and many insects, such as the Pine Sawfly, find a mate, and the female lays her eggs. Birds such as Goldcrests and Capercaillies feed their young on some of these insects.

As in a broadleaved wood, many young mammals grow up and learn how to find food.

Feeding on pines

Fully grown caterpillar

The Pine Hawk Moth caterpillar hatches in summer and feeds on Scots Pine needles. It prefers the older needles.

Insect food

Ball of insect food is passed to the young.

Nightjars live on the edge of pinewoods.

The Nightjar catches flying insects for its young. It scoops them up in its wide open mouth as it flies along.

A Pine wood in summer

Parent **Crossbills** cough up partly digested pine seeds to feed to the young.

Scots Pine tree →

Young **Pine Martens** often go with their mother on hunting trips and learn to catch voles and small birds.

Juniper fruits are developing over the summer.

Bilberry bushes have blue-black berries in mid-summer.

Lesser Twayblade

These **Pinewood plants** flower in summer.

Tormentil

Chickweed Wintergreen

Autumn

Broadleaved Woods

As the days shorten and the temperature drops, most of the trees and shrubs lose their leaves. Their nuts and berries are ripe and provide an important source of food for birds and animals. Many fungi produce fruiting bodies at this time of year.

Most of the young birds and mammals that were born in summer are fully grown and independent of their parents. Many of the young birds will migrate to warmer climates where there is plenty of food.

Stinkhorn fungi

The strong smell of the slime attracts flies.

The spores of this fungus are produced in a dark slime on the head of the stem. Flies eat the slime and help to disperse the spores.

Seed dispersal

Dogwood
Birds eat the berries and fly away. The seeds are dispersed in the birds' droppings.

Ash
The coat around the seed expands to form a wing. This carries the seed away on the wind.

Beech
Animals, such as Squirrels, store these nuts. Uneaten nuts may grow into new trees.

Seeds may be dispersed by the wind, water or by animals. They stand more chance of surviving away from competition with other plants.

An Oak wood in autumn

Blue Tits search the trees and bushes for insects, spiders and seeds.

Jays eat nuts and berries in autumn. They also collect nuts, especially acorns, and bury them in the litter.

The **Grey Squirrel** feeds on nuts, berries and fungi. It makes stores of nuts in the ground, in tree hollows or in its drey (nest).

The **Hazel** nuts are ripe and fall off the tree.

The **Roe Deer** start to grow a thicker coat ready for winter. The males cast their antlers.

More **Woodcock** arrive from Scandinavia to join the resident birds in the wood.

Bullfinches may eat **Honeysuckle** berries.

The **Hedgehog** searches in the leaf litter for worms, beetles and other small creatures.

Honey Fungus

At the end of autumn, the **White Admiral Butterfly** caterpillar wraps a **Honeysuckle** leaf around itself like a small cocoon.

Earthstar

Many **fungi** produce fruiting bodies, especially in wet weather.

Penny Bun

OCTOBER 5TH.
Hazel nuts eaten by
birds and mammals.

Sycamore

Oak

Beech

Autumn
leaves

Bank
Vole

Bird

Split by
Squirrel

Fungi

Penny Bun has
pores under cap.

Sulphur Tuft
has gills
under
cap

You could collect leaves, feathers and nuts in autumn. Draw or stick them into your diary.

Ivy is one of the few plants which flowers in autumn. It is pollinated by insects, such as flies and wasps.

Bumble Bees in autumn

Queen Bee

Queen Bee

The worker bees and drones left behind all die.

The new queens leave the nest. They will not lay their eggs until the following spring.

Coniferous Woods

With the coming of autumn, the plants and animals prepare for the harsh winter months ahead. Some shrubs, such as Bilberry, lose their leaves, and most ferns and other plants on the woodland floor die back.

Migrant birds leave for their winter feeding grounds. The birds and animals that remain eat as much as possible or set aside food stores.

Ospreys

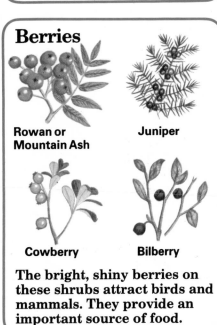

Adult **Ospreys** leave before the young.

In autumn, Ospreys fly from parts of Europe to North Africa where the weather is warmer and there are plenty of fish for them to eat.

Berries

Rowan or Mountain Ash

Juniper

Cowberry

Bilberry

The bright, shiny berries on these shrubs attract birds and mammals. They provide an important source of food.

A Pine wood in autumn

Scots Pine tree →

The **Crossbill** uses its curved beak to force the scales on pine cones apart. It licks out the seeds with its horny tongue.

Pine Martens may eat a lot of fruit in autumn including the berries on the pinewood shrubs.

Juniper berries are ripe from September to October.

Bilberry berries are ripe from July to September.

The fruiting bodies of many **fungi** grow up through the litter.

Boletus Fungus

False Chanterelle

Winter

Broadleaved Woods

The short winter days and long, bitterly cold nights make conditions very harsh for plants and animals. The birds that remain in the wood often feed in mixed flocks. They spend most of the daylight hours searching for insect eggs or pupae hidden under tree bark or in the leaf litter.

Mammals that stay active all winter have thick winter coats while birds fluff out their feathers or roost together to keep warm.

Hibernation

The **Dormouse** spends the winter in a deep sleep (hibernation) because there is very little food for it to eat. The stores of fat in its body keep it alive.

Winter buds

Ash

Beech

Silver Birch

Sycamore

You can identify trees in winter by looking at the shape and arrangement of buds. The tough outer scales of the bud protect the young leaves and flowers that are inside.

An Oak wood in winter

Jays find many of the food stores they made in autumn and eat the nuts they buried.

Blue Tits usually feed with other small birds, such as **Treecreepers** and **Great Tits**.

Roe Deer shelter in the wood, sometimes in small groups. They feed on **Bramble**.

Treecreeper

Male **Hazel** catkins open to shed their pollen in late winter.

The **Hedgehog** hibernates inside a special nest made of leaves and grass.

Great Tit

The **Woodcock** spends a lot of time probing in the mud for Earthworms with its long beak.

The **White Admiral Butterfly** caterpillar hibernates inside its protective leaf case.

Bank Voles tunnel under the snow to feed on plant leaves and roots.

JANUARY 14TH

Trees looked very green

Green on wettest side of trees.

Tracks in the snow

Sharp claw prints— probably a fox track.

Galls pecked by birds.

Make sketches of any tracks you find in the snow or mud. Measure the tracks and try to identify them.

The **Grey Squirrel** has a thicker, silvery grey coat in winter. It has white tufts behind its ears and a white fringe around its tail.

Ivy berries develop over the winter from flowers that were fertilized in autumn.

Bumble Bees in winter

Queen Bumble Bees hibernate over the winter in dead wood, leaf litter or underground.

Coniferous Woods

As most of the trees keep their leaves in winter, conifer woods help to protect the wildlife from the worst of the winter weather. However, many conifer woods grow in cold places and there may be a thick layer of snow on the ground. This helps to keep the plants warm but makes it harder for mammals such as deer to find food. They have to dig through the snow to feed.

Pine Processionary Moths

These moths are not found in Britain.

Caterpillars of the Pine Processionary Moth spin silk nests to protect them from cold winter weather. On fine days, they come out to feed.

Winter coat

Stoat in summer

The Stoat often has a white coat in winter. This helps it to blend into a snowy background and protects it from enemies, such as Foxes.

A Pine wood in winter

The female **Crossbill** collects pine twigs, mosses and lichens to build her nest. She lays two to five eggs in late winter.

Scots Pine tree

The **Pine Marten** is active all winter because it can still find voles and small birds to eat.

Juniper is an evergreen shrub and keeps its leaves all year round.

Bilberry twigs are bare of leaves all winter.

Red Deer tracks

31

Index

Books to read

Exploring Woods. Peter Schofield (Independent Television Books)
Nature's Hidden World, Woods & Forests. Edited by Michael Chinery, Written by Michel Cuisin (Ward Lock)
Exploring the Woodland. Leslie Jackman (Evans)
Woodlands. William Condry (Collins)
The Forest World. Eric Duffey (Orbis)
On Nature's Trail. Ken Hoy (Mitchell Beazley)
Trees in the Wild. Gerald Wilkinson (John Bartholomew)
Trees and Woodlands in the British Landscape. Oliver Rackham (Dent)
Woodland Birds. Eric Simms (Collins)
The Countryside in Spring, Summer, Autumn, Winter. E. A. Ellis (Jarrold)

The Family Naturalist. Michael Chinery (Macdonald and Jane's)
Nocturnals. Editor Malcolm Ellis (Dent)

Clubs and societies

The Royal Society for Nature Conservation (RSNC) will give you more information about the county **Nature Conservation Trusts** which have a common junior club **Watch**. This is for 8 to 15 year olds who are interested in nature and the environment. Write to: 22 The Green, Nettleham, Lincoln, LN2 2NR.
The Nature Conservancy Council (NCC) will supply lists of **National (and local) Nature Reserves** as well as leaflets and other educational material. Write to: Calthorpe House, Calthorpe Street, Banbury, Oxon, OX16 8EX.

The Council for Environmental Conservation (CoEnCo) will supply addresses of local Natural History Societies. Write to: Zoological Gardens Regent's Park, London NW1 4RY (Pleas enclose s.a.e.)
The Young Ornithologists Club (YOC) is the junior wing of the **Royal Society for the Protection of Birds (RSPB)**. Membe can take part in birdwatching outings, projects and holiday courses. Write to: The Lodge, Sandy, Beds, SG19 2DL.
The RSPCA organizes field courses and lectures on natural history. Write to: Education Department, Causeway, Horsham, Sussex.
The Woodland Trust, Westgate, Grantham, Lincs, NG31 6LL.
Forestry Commission, Information Branch, 235, Corstorphine Road, Edinburgh, EH12 7AT.